Pi Masten
10/26/'84

This book
belongs to –

CLAIRE K. LANGHAM
Intercultural Training and Consulting

Teaching Assistant Development Program, B-033
UNIVERSITY OF CALIFORNIA, SAN DIEGO
La Jolla, California 92093

Area Code 619
452-6767

the DESERTED ROOSTER

by RIC MASTEN

SUNFLOWER INK
Palo Colorado Canyon
Carmel, Calif. 93923

NICHOLS & DIMES

The book was produced by NICHOLS & DIMES, 1025 West 15th Street, Odessa, Texas. 79763.

(paperback) 9 8 7 6 5 4 3 2 1

Library of Congress Catalogue Card No. 82-60672

ISBN 931104-11-4

for men who
    are headed into it
    in it
    or have made it through

ACKNOWLEDGMENTS

Special thanks to Cynthia Clack who helped select the poems included here, not understanding a word she read.

I must also acknowledge that my daughter April Masten (Di Girolamo) has read these poems and says she understand everything. Adding that if I use the subtitle *"and other things a woman wouldn't understand"* she will know her father has resorted to bullshit chauvinist PR.

My wife Billie Barbara, however, states that for thirty years my behavior has always remained a mystery to her.

The poems in this collection were selected from the books *Speaking poems, Stark Naked, Voice of the Hive, His & Hers* and *Even As We Speak.* All were published by SUNFLOWER INK.

preface

Because Ric Masten is a poet more to be heard than read, he is necessarily a road poet, meaning he operates on a timetable like that of a truck gardener. Periods spent at home growing things alternate with road tours during which he distributes them and gathers the seeds for the next growing season. He is never livlier, never keener than when on these trips, and so it is only natural that he was on the road this spring when the idea for this book ran over him.

The first time I had ever seen such a collision was two years ago. I was slumped sluggishly at a typewriter, staring into its works and hoping the telephone wouldn't ring when it did. It was Ric, and it was apparent from the tone of his voice that something had just sideswiped him.

"Hey, Kisling!" he cried in that voice he uses to raise wage slaves from the dead. "Hey, I made it, man!"

"Hullo, Ric," I said, stirring slightly. "What do you mean you made it?"

"I'm fifty years old," he chirped. "I made it!"

And I got it. At the time I was three months away from my own fiftieth birthday, running on automatic pilot, and without warning this itinerant troubador was on the blower with urgent news, to-wit: "I just found out it can be done!" Masten has a gift for getting the drop on people that way. In fact, he does some of his best work from ambush—catching you when you're on the verge of swearing that you're not now and never have been a member of the human race, then popping up with the startling suggestion that you may be able to change your defense at the last minute, come right out and admit your humanity and thus avoid the unpleasantness of an insanity plea.

The first time he blindsides you you're tempted to attribute it to wizardry. The next time you're not so sure. You begin to suspect you're dealing with a man who pays so much attention to his own internal weather that he's picked up a few hints about yours, too.

Thus I wasn't totally unprepared when, early in May of this year, after winding up a whirling dervish three-day engagement in Denver, Ric rang my phone early on the morning he was scheduled to leave town for his home in Big Sur, California.

"Hey!" he said. "Let's write a book."

Sideswiped again. It was like having a friend get you by the lapel and say "Hey, I've gotta leave town in about five minutes, but I was just thinking maybe it would be a good idea if we discovered penicillin or something."

"What kind of book?" I inquired.

"A book about the deserted rooster," said Ric. "A book of poems women won't understand."

"It should be a great seller," I said. "Every woman in the world will buy one."

"Yeah," he replied, ignoring that possibility and plunging on into the land of the deserted rooster, that nervous old bird who has arrived at his awkward years—that time of life when he's too young to retire, too old to throw it all up and run away to Tahiti and too proud to admit that anything is wrong. "He's been neglected," said Ric. And so he has.

Considering the number of survival manuals currently available in occupied America, it is odd that one hasn't yet been offered for this deserted rooster. We have numerous how-to books for downtrodden wives, parents, children, minority groups. We have books of advice for getting ahead, managing money, protecting investments, winning at the office, winning on Wall Street, winning at home, winning video games, winning on the tennis court, winning in bed, living alone, living together, living in the city, living in the woods. There are books explaining how to get married, divorced, remarried, redivorced, involved or uninvolved. But so far the care and feeding of the deserted rooster has been overlooked.

At this point some Ms. is likely to say: whoa, there, rooster. What do you mean by "poems that women won't understand?" Haven't women been patronized enough without someone suggesting that? Ye Gods. What kind of chauvinist would even imply such a thing in these liberated times? Could this be the work of a man who's looking for a rap on the head with an umbrella? Or the ramblings of some macho dolt who hasn't sense enough to come in out of the rain?

Your indulgence a moment, Ms.

Consider that if everyone had sense enough to come in out of the rain the umbrella never would have been invented. But it was invented, and no doubt by a man. He probably was a man who believed that the age-old problem of getting wet outdoors could be solved once and for all with a little portable tent.

Isn't that the kind of approach you might expect from a man? Of course it is. He would strive to be logical about it. Practical. He would get some wire and cloth and a few springs and hinges and put together a folding contraption that could be quickly erected to ward off raindrops.

How might a woman tackle the same problem? Since she knows perfectly well that the human skin is waterproof by nature, she might not tackle it at all. She might not even see it as a problem. Instead she might suggest to her hyperkinetic spouse, as he struggles with cloth and wire and pliers to invent the umbrella, that he quit tinkering with that silly looking thing and go out for groceries before it rains. She might even say to him: "I don't understand what you think you're doing with all that stuff."

"Of course you don't," he replies. "Women never understand." And he labors on past dusk into the gathering night, damaging his eyesight, missing his supper and growing so irritable that he finally cries to his wife, "For God's sake, will you get those kids out of here while I'm trying to invent?"

Days, perhaps months later, he leaps up from his workbench, brandishing the world's first umbrella and crying: "I did it! I did it!" Immediately he calls in the guy next door, shows him the umbrella and says, "Look!"

The neighbor inspects the contraption, opens it, closes it, and quickly grasps its significance. "Well I'll be damned!" he says. "An umbrella!" To his wife, who has come along with him to see what all the excitement is about, he says: "Look, honey! George has just invented the umbrella!"

"The what?" she asks, eyeing the thing in much the same way George's wife did.

"You wouldn't understand," says George. "My wife didn't either." How could a woman understand that through his enterprise and inspiration one of the world's long-standing problems has been solved?

"Just wait 'til the next time it rains," says George. "You'll see." Grinning, he snaps the umbrella erect. "See, you just hold it like this and it keeps the rain off you wherever you go. What do you think of that?"

"I'm not too big on the color," says his wife. "Does it have to be black? Couldn't it be something more cheerful? Yellow, or light green or something?"

"That doesn't make any difference," says George, growing a little impatient. "What's the color got to do with it?"

"You wouldn't understand," replies his wife.

Wouldn't understand indeed, says George, but not out loud. As far as he's concerned it's the other way around. It's women who don't understand men's enterprises. And he hasn't got time to explain it all to her because he has other umbrellas to invent.

The truth of it is, Ms., that there are millions of Georges out there, madly inventing umbrellas and not worrying much about who understands and who doesn't until, sometime between the ages of 40 and 60, a disturbing thought begins to creep in. George finds that after all those years of ruining his eyesight, missing meals and shooing the kids out of the workshop, in his fervor to make a living, provide a home, get ahead, inventing isn't as absorbing as it used to be. Why, he asks himself, is he still turning out umbrellas for a world that seems more and more to be coming in out of the rain?

George is the deserted rooster. He's a man who was bred for the cockpit of competition, tempered by years of scuffling in the marketplace, and even though he's scratched out enough success to crow about, he's running a little scared, feeling a little tired. You've noticed that his plumage has faded and thinned on top, haven't you? Well, he's noticed that you've noticed, and it bugs him. But he keeps silent because he's a tough old bird and tough old birds aren't supposed to make little peeping noises.

Ever since he was a kid he has been a go-getter, and now that he's gone and gotten he's not certain which way to go next. Some of his kids are out going and getting and others of them don't seem to be going anywhere or to be much concerned about it. He said nothing when his wife signed up for a consciousness-raising course, but now that she's absorbed in that, there isn't anybody left to shoo out of the workshop. What the hell is going on here?

He is beset by a vague sinking feeling and nagged by a belief he brought with him from boyhood—that it's all right for the women and children to flee into new roles. They're perfectly welcome to pile into their liberated lifeboats and paddle away, relying on their champions to tell them which way the shore lies and how to steer for it. But he's spent his life being the captain, and the captain is supposed to go down with the ship, isn't he?

At this point Ric Masten darts out of the thicket and cries "No. He doesn't have to if he doesn't want to. After all, he *is* the captain, isn't he?"

This is good news for deserted roosters, made even better by knowing it is being brought to them by an old captain whose own feet are slightly awash. Who inspires a balding man's trust and confidence better than another balding man?

We mustn't assume, however, that the poems of Ric Masten in this book constitute a Chilton's maintenance guide for making older-model males easier to start in the mornings. These poems are not performance oriented. Rather they are an account, carefully kept over the years, of the gradual dawning in a man of the knowledge that he isn't going to live forever, and the even more important knowledge that this big news isn't exactly news to the rest of the world.

Long before Ric's concept of the deserted rooster had hatched into anything like a chronology, he wrote *The Second Half* (Page 7.)

Over the dozen years since that was written, a certain few of Ric's other poems have addressed that perplexed rooster's dilemma, and little by little the account has unfolded with the kinetic certainty of a multiplication table.

Here was a rooster growing older, but there was in that an unmistakable passion. Not a mere longing to stay alive, because anybody, given average metabolism and a little luck, can do that. Rather these poems express a passion for *being* alive. The sequence is itself the song, and on that morning in May when Ric telephoned, it was clear that he was ready to sing it.

Many of these poems are as lighthearted as jokes, and like jokes, they hit because there is this kicker: who is the joke on, anyway? Another of Ric's gifts is the dressing of truth in jokes' clothing, then having a good laugh on himself, the gentle inference being that if you got it, perhaps the joke's on you, too. You and Ric.

I saw that very thing happen this spring when Ric talked before the Denver Rotary Club, rooster to rooster. As he once observed, "to be a poet reading is chancy work at best."

To be a bearded man preparing to pull a poem on a room full of 500 Rotarians is chancier still. It's not unlike the TV commercial where somebody pulls a six pack of light beer on truck drivers.

The first verse he pulled was about going bald (page 70). It began:

"Getting a little thin on top, aren't you, sport?"

The poem was flipped off as neatly and easily as a bit of ice from the top of a can. Then he quickly popped another verse and handed it to them. One about battle fatigue in the middle ages. After that came perhaps a dozen more, poems about the feminist movement, the emptiness that comes with career success, an ageing man's need for sexual assurance, and the remorse of a father who realizes belatedly he's spent too much time with his work and not enough with his children.

His audience of Rotary roosters gradually began to resemble the TV truck drivers tentatively swallowing light beer as if to say that even though this stuff went down pretty smoothly, it had a real kick to it, too. Ric never suggests that we're all in this together, nor that we're all in this alone. Instead he reminds us, and his poems confirm it, that we're not alone alone.

What follows are the poems themselves. In the dozen years over which they were written—and spoken—Ric has lived through his lugubrious forties, skidded on into his fifties, seen his four children grow up and go out into the world, plunged with his wife Billie Barbara into a shattering marriage crisis at the 25-year mark, and with her emerged undaunted if not unscathed. So it is not as if he leaped up on the spur of the notion this spring and announced: "I shall put together a book about the special problems which nag the middle-aged man." Not at all. He has been hatching this one all along, marking off each milestone and each millstone as they pass. Taken together, they say to the deserted rooster: "The end is not yet, old bird. Keep scratchin'."

Jack Kisling
Denver, Colorado
June 1982

contents

Over 50

author's note

All that follows was written since I turned forty. However, rather than present the material in the exact chronological order in which it was written, I have chosen to group the poems in the period of my life **(40 to 45, 45 to 50 and OVER 50)** where the incidents happened and the insights came.

And as always, my poetry is meant to be spoken out loud. This book is intended to be a joint venture so read it to someone or find someone to read it to you. This way everything means twice as much.

the
DESERTED
ROOSTER

THE DESERTED ROOSTER

if this were a documentary
lorne green would narrate
describing in his big male-animal-world way
the migration
as one by one the fledglings flew the coop
followed by the hen
liberated and running off to join the sisters
cloistered in the halls
of a community college
singing

> gloria
> gloria
> steinem—till it becomes catholic

so far nothing new
children leaving home
a woman's victory
over the empty nest syndrome
themes done to death

but the deserted rooster is a subject
that has not yet been addressed
we know him
only as that laughable old strutter
preening and parading up and down
involved in his sexual prowess
and the sound of his own voice
up
at an ungodly hour to start the day
it was all part of the job

and there wasn't a problem
when there wasn't a choice

but picture him now
after the exodus
all alone
scratching around in his abandoned domain
looking for a good reason to get up tomorrow
and crow

if this were a documentary
it would end
focused on a stereotype weather vane
rusted on the turning point

     in a changing wind

40 to 45

THE SECOND HALF

i turned forty a while ago
and came dribbling out of the locker room
ready to start the second half
glancing up at the scoreboard
i saw that we were behind
      7 to 84
and it came to me then
      we ain't gonna win
and considering the score
i'm beginning to be damn glad
this particular game ain't gonna go on
      forever

but don't take this to mean i'm ready
for the showers
take it to mean i'm probably gonna play
one hellava second half

i told this to some kids in the court
next to mine and they laughed
but i don't think they understood
      how could they
playing in the first quarter only one point
      behind

ELLEN AND I

my youngest daughter
likes to ride
to the mailbox with me

she fetches the mail
while i turn the car around
then she climbs into the back seat

and doles out my letters
slowly
inspecting each envelope

till i am infuriated
and turn red
and shout at her

ellen!
gimme
the letters!

my youngest daughter likes to do this
it is one of the few times
she has my full attention

THE WEANING

after considerable work in the field
i have come to the conclusion
that when it comes to me
and my children
it is easy to say "no" all the time
and it is easy to say "yes" all the time
but it is impossible
to be a logical consistent parent

however
i do not lie awake nights
over this any longer
for to treat children
in a logical consistent fashion
and then turn them out into the world
as we know it
would be a cruel crippling inhuman thing to do

it is only fair though
that when the kids have broken loose
and are out on their own
they should receive a hand-written letter
from me their father
expressing my love
and stating that all is forgiven
if they promise not to come home

THE PROJECTIONIST

(When the creative urge has no place
to go, it backs up and under pressure
is transformed into anxiety.)

it happens like this
i being a salesman of sorts
am out on the road
peddling rhyme and a theory of time
to other men's sons while mine back home
falls in among those
who deal in junk and
      steal and
      have dirty fingernails
      you know the type
then at the wheel of a car he swiped
the inevitable chase
the hair-raising ride
      to the killing ground
where like bonnie and clyde
he's brought down by the law
      to die in the dust
      of a backwoods road
      screaming the name of his pa
while i'm on stage in milwaukee
receiving your gracious applause

      you know i ought to become
      a suspense and horror movie producer
      spending as much time as i do
      in the projection booth
      scaring myself to death
      with my own warped imagination
      in bed before it's time to get up
      is when i do my best work

using that gray
empty space
to screen the rushes
of plot possibilities
cranking out sordid little gems like:
because a vegetarian told her
not to put chemicals into her body
my scatterbrained daughter
goes off the pill
gets pregnant
and then three months along
ill with german measles
too proud to phone us and ask for help
she runs off to wander
the cold
hard streets of the city
along and penniless
selling her blood for money
to pay the abortionist fee
while i'm away in new england
making poems under a tree

or maybe i see myself
so involved in my work
my wife starved for affection
goes out and joins an encounter group
having a real gut experience
and shortly thereafter runs off
with the leader a
kissy huggy long-haired creep
who wears a mexican sarape
and a five-pound ankh around his neck
using the group grope technique
to recruit good christian women
to come work
in his san francisco massage parlor

and sometimes when i really get going
i can follow the story line
clear to the end
where the music swells
and i see myself old
     and tired
     and feeble
dying in the men's room
of a greyhound bus station
a ticket to pocatello idaho in my hand

now everyone knows
it takes a certain amount of
     drama
     suspense
     and tragedy
to keep life interesting
but this is ridiculous

AN OLD SKIN GAME

when you tried to pick my wife up
that night
i didn't put you down
like i would have some white dude
oh no
i wouldn't want you
to think i was prejudiced

man
you sure musta been tired of me
reachin' out to shake your hand
actin' like you didn't have one

tippy toein' 'round your shadow
grinnin'
with my eyes lookin' off to one side
tryin' not to see
that somethin' was wrong
when nothin' really was

so you had to go
and grow your own hand back
with no help from me
makin' it into a fist
and holdin' that fist so high
i couldn't help but admire it

now i know
you've been about the business
of your own escape to freedom

not mine
but you left a hole in the fence
and i got loose too

so
thanks to you
the next time you mess with my wife
i will be able
to treat you like a man

*(Trying to get a line on racist tendencies of mine, I discover
what a sexist I really am.)*

A SMALL QUIET WAR

and she's at it again—my wife
under the house
digging

i can hear her down there
with my old rusty tools
picking and shovelling away
hollowing out a place
for her imagination
to run wild in

she's been at it off and on now
for two years
running back and forth
with one shovel full of dirt at a time
throwing it into the yard
doing it the hard way
and i must admit i'm always surprised
and a bit annoyed
when i see the size of the pile
she is making
but it's her project
and she says
i'm not and don't have to be
involved

still and all
it has now become impossible for me
to lie here comfortably
listening to the ball game

TO CHOKE

is when the story goes well
the one you dearly love to tell
the flock responding
as you bring them toward the finale
racing about like a clever boarder collie

but this evening
there is something in the wind
a crumb
a trace of wheat thin
something sucked in
to lodge between the verb and synonym
and the silence that follows
is not golden

and when neither wine or water
will touch it
helplessly you turn the story
over to your wife to finish
knowing she never found it
particularly amusing

and also knowing
that while you sit there in tears
strangling
she will be getting
twice as many laughs as you would have
simply by mangling the punch line

and that's what really sticks in your craw

ON VACATION

well—i bet we'd stop if it were you
who needed a service station!

not true—not true
says i to her boiling over
but driving through from dawn till dusk
grim as death—whipped along
by some primal hunting urge
to find the meat—kill it
and get it safely home

like all the desperate men i've seen
inching their machine along the california coast
i carry on
one eye on the calendar the other on the map
at the wheel but never feeling in the driver's seat

missing everything
except the double line
that hauls me through a Rand McNally
nightmare
and leaves me sick with fear
hearing nothing but a queer sound in the engine
the obvious click—click—click click
that she puts down as my imagination
suggesting that perhaps the battery
needs lubrication
when the time comes
i always take my leave like bitter medicine
watching the signs fly by

counting the miles and minutes off
praying that nothing goes wrong
till i'm back where i belong—on the job

caught up again
in a seemingly endless exhausting work year
made bearable only
by the prospect of another summer
on vacation

COMING AND GOING

i have noticed
that men
somewhere around forty
tend to come in from the field
with a sigh
and removing their coat in the hall
call into the kitchen

> you were right
> grace
> it ain't out there
> just like you've always said

and she
with the children gone at last
breathless
puts her hat on her head

> the hell it ain't

coming and going
they pass
in the doorway

DAMN YOU GAUGUIN
AND ALL OTHER WHITE WHALES

for someone caught in the paper claw
of a corporate world
the watercolor
hanging in his office
was good enough to be terribly distracting
he had talent alright
enough to keep one small part of his mind
          waving free
like ahab's arm
beckoning from that elusive dream

          but how do you ask an orthodontist
          to take the bands off the kid's teeth
          i mean
          do you go to him and say
          remove the braces dr. bently
          i'm running off to the islands
          to be an artist
          i can't afford them anymore
          or do you get a pair of pliers
          and do it yourself

the young and romantic
might find this hard to believe
but you simply cannot get to tahiti from here

MY BARN

i pause in the road
and look back to my barn
a shed really
but it is mine
and i say it's a barn

i can see where the new nails
shine in the braille of weathered wood
well wintered wood
snatched from the path
of a mindless caterpillar

i played the priest and preacher
with those unhappy planks
and salvaged every stick i could
and stood them up again
to be my barn

but now — pausing in the road
i am uneasy
my apron is heavy with these idle nails
and yet back there my barn is built
and i have all this time to kill

COURTING DISASTER

sometimes i let the everyday mail
the bills and propositions
push me to a place
where i would welcome
a calamity of nature

      a wildfire
      out of control
      raging through
      the piles of collected junk
      i can't get rid of
      razing all that i have
      except the opportunity
      to begin again

perhaps a catastrophic flood
sweeping away a life
that has become a complicated nuisance
leaving behind an acre
of straightforward mud and muck
to deal with

or best of all an earthquake
shaking me out
of this unreasonable depression
a seismic upheaval
large enough to level everything
      and replace it
      with something real
      to dig out from under

all of us
left in the aftermath
with coffee in a paper cup
talking it over around a red cross truck
        how awful
        how wonderful

along the san andreas fault
you'd be surprised
how many of us there are
secretly hoping

THE ANNUAL CHECK UP

every now and then i discover this
       strange lump
in my abdomen which i finger
when no one is looking to see if
       the soreness
is still there and it always is
and so in fear and trembling i go
to see my doctor and hear
       the bad news
and this kindly old bird hops around me
like a crow with a piece of tin foil
poking and peering
until stroking his chin he declares
that i am in A-1 condition and if i'd stop
handling my pancreas it wouldn't be
       so sore

and yet always in the end
i leave his office with the certain knowledge
that i will be
       dead
in six months the good doctor keeping my
       awful infirmities
from me so that i can enjoy what little time
i have left and bravely with this information
hidden under my coat i return hom
to be with my family and together
we climb the hill in back of the house
to sit a spell
and really watch a cloud move

i guess you'd say
i was a bit of a hypochondriac and that's OK
it keeps me close to things
and on this ward we are all
        terminal
anyway

THE TOWER

i had a vision once of a tower
here on the shoulder of this mountain
and i became a wildman with a hammer
and a dream
but don't be overly impressed with men
who build towers
there are any number of journeyman
carpenters
and stonemasons
that can tell you how to do it

the building part is easy
it's the living in it that comes hard

with some simple instruction
anyone can hang a door
but if you know the art of oiling hinges
teach me

THE PRISONERS

though i have seen the photographs
of those ragged weary men
still i think i envy them
the prisoners
captured in a good

         and holy war
which every war has been

caught and confined
by an obviously evil enemy
left to rot in some forgotten
prison camp
stubbornly clinging to secret information
for which i'd rather die than tell
surviving in a roach and rat-infested cell
my eye fixed
on that thin sliver of hope
at the edge of the door
the crack of light
         that keeps us alive
in our solitary confinement

yes — there have been times
i've wished it were a simpler prison
for out here
in this open field of sunshine
it is far
     far more difficult
     to plan the great escape

45 to 50

the women are organizing in the kitchen
they want a living wage for housework
and one of them
has it figured in such a way
the government would pay
which might be OK
until you consider coming home
at the end of a hard day
to find
               a teamster at the sink

CIRCUS MAXIMUS

reaching for a mile she is
hoping for an inch she was
burning her bra
while the cameras pan the crooked smile
on the face of a nervous man
probably henpecked most of his life
the entire spectacle
making good copy i guess
in the chauvinist press

but aside from the rhetoric
and the upraised fist
the central theme of the feminist
was best expressed in a speech
delivered from a double bed
when after twenty years of marriage
my wife said

        the economics of the ERA
        will allow me
        to stay with you
        not because i have to
        but because
        and only because i want to

and this power play more than any other
has the gladiators huddled
beneath the colosseum floor
clinging to the urinal
in much the same way early christians
clung to their cross

but in the words of one true believer
waiting to be flung
to the lions

        brother
        you must admit
        these are sure exciting times

TAP ROOTS

hunkered down back there in the half light
before the dawn when i couldn't see so good
looking out from under a shelf-life brow
i would watch her
      with the child
      with the life
      SHE
      had created

now this was before the word
and because i knew not the why of it
nor the how
i was filled with envy and rage
and i hated her
for try as i might
strain as i would
i the male
could create nothing more impressive
      than a turd

wasn't i bigger'n her and stronger
and so to cover my chagrin and disgrace
i gave her a cuff across the face
took up a spear
and walked out into the morning

be patient with me woman
i'm working on it
but when the tap root
goes down that deep into history

the tree is not easily moved
and now that you do have your sperm bank
and have mastered karate

    have i become irrelevant again?
    or just plain paranoid

THE HYPOTHETICAL QUESTION

lies beside the road like a stone
and probably should be left entirely alone
it being hypothetical
should we bother with what we uncover
while turning it over?

suppose i should ask you
what you think you would do
if all other humans suddenly vanished
leaving you the last of mankind
and with the knowledge that you are the absolute
end of the line
everything else intact though
      supermarkets — libraries
      gas stations — animals
      everything
just as you'd find it today
      minus people

alone
confronting this situation
do you think you'd commit suicide then and there
without hesitation
or do you think you couldn't do that
but most likely you'd wither away
going out of your mind in a very short time
or are you someone who thinks you could
live your life out combing beaches
      a dog at your side — a stick in your hand
      like robinson crusoe

only this time with no hope of finding
        friday's prints in the sand

in short
how much do you think you need your fellow man?
well
        ask a hypothetical question
        get a hypothetical answer

or so i thought
till i was surprised and brought
down in flames
by a braless young girl
a hard line feminist who took aim and said

        boy —
        if i were the one in the problem you posed
        i would not commmit suicide
        comb beaches
        nor would i wither away
        those are the options of a male chauvinist
        pig

        rather
        i would head for the nearest sperm bank
        and being a healthy female
        impregnate myself
        and start it all over again
        thanks to science this time minus
        men

like i said the hypothetical question
lies beside the road like a stone
and probably should be left entirely alone
but turn it over and usually the usual number
        of salamanders — sowbugs

and centipedes will be uncovered
but look out
for an occasional black widow spider
who kills and devours her mate
a fact
that is not in the least bit hypothetical
and in a funny science fiction sort of way
food for thought

right fellas?

FREE AT LAST

if she's part of the movement
she no longer wants to be a girl
        a chick
        or a broad
        not even a lady
she's a feminist
a liberated woman and i'm for this
a free female
means a free male
free enough to openly express
my childish insecurity

        if a person
wants to whine and whimper
now-a-days a person can
but every time i do
my liberated woman says
        act like a man

STOP ME IF YOU'VE HEARD IT

a story always looses something
in the second telling
and so
        over the years gladys & j. grabowski
developed a relationship
that needed a third party around
to break the silence
        when the children behaved
        the job secure
        if no one had died
        and the car didn't knock
they lived with the sound of the traffic outside
and the clock

        gladys survived
with the jr. league and a brownie troop
and when the kids grew up she went into group
        j. held on playing golf
till his back wouldn't let him
then feeling his age one day
left home and flew to cleveland on business
checking into a motel
as mr. & mrs. smith
but like the sales pitch says
        after one night in a holiday inn
        you'll not be surprised in the next

in retrospect
i think the grabowski affair
was a kind of suicide attempt

on something gone humdrum
and he going to sleep that night
vaguely wondered
if the maid would arrive in time to turn off the gas
       if she did
       perhaps it would be a good omen
if not —
well a story always looses something
in the second telling

AN IMPOSSIBLE AFFAIR

to see a length of time through
to its conclusion
with someone close
can be a ripping business
for the end is always in sight
approaching relentlessly
the clock a death head
ever present — grinning
   a sure winner

from the start the action and closing lines
      memorized
me tearing myself
from the grip of your young eyes
stumbling off stage blind and bleeding
clinging to dreams of brave gypsy children
riding the crest of the wind whipped now
singing
   i am alive
   and i know it
it was an impossible affair
and that
was exactly what i loved about it

i
who had just entered the rapids
of estrangement
was most interested in what she might say
she
who had just come through the white water
the wild water
the mad crazy part of the river
      now tell me
      for the past few years
      have you encouraged your dear spouse
      to get with it
      and find herself
      and be an entity unto herself?
yes
      and did she do it
      i mean go out and find something of value
      aside from the house
      the children
      and you?
yes
      now tell me
      this strange young unexplainable
      new object of your affection
      is she mostly a pool
      for you to reflect upon?
i would hope there is more to it than that
but
well — yes   shit!
              she said

MY GOD! TO BE A HOUSEWIFE

i have in my life stepped out on my wife and tried
          waiting
in a white room
for a young working woman
to bring me color through a white door
it has been a long morning
with this blank piece of paper
and quiet guitar
the sun came crawling on the floor
and i watched it with no more on my mind
than you and this
          slow unwinding lonely time

you will come soon for lunch
i will hear your sound in the hall
your hand on the latch and then time will fly
till you're off to work again
and i am left alone again
washing the afternoon walls with my eyes
my god! to be a housewife waiting
          always waiting
and you can't create while waiting
          you can only wait

(This painful experience taught me that time does not pass
as slowly for a hunter hunting as it does for the one waiting
for the hunters return. Most men, being hunters are not in
touch with this.)

MR. CENTERFOLD

a self-righteous
pseudo-perceptive woman once told me
that there had never been
a middle-aged man
who had gone to the trouble of losing
a great deal of over-weight
who
at the same time
wasn't having a secret affair

      or planning to

if you don't believe me
she said
just watch mr. centerfold on parade
marching sideways
to the bathroom mirror

now
a sweeping statement like that
is the thing in this world
i hate most of all
except perhaps
knowing that i have just been nailed to the wall

ECONOMIC INDICATORS

            part time yard work
            inquire after dark

            waitress wanted
            for interview
            call the naked lunch

have you ever applied for work
you didn't want
and would never take
just to find out
if you really had an ace in the hole

operating out of some knee-jerk
sense of self preservation
showing your stuff
throwing your best sunday punch
into the phone
only to be told
you weren't right for the job

have you ever let yourself
get caught short like this?
winding up wiped out

well i have   and now
                 a few words
                 about the great depression

STRESS

i have just hung up the telephone
but the bad news will have to wait
        right now
        i must deal with the lump of tension
        that has just been thrust into my body
        like a frankfurter into a sliced roll

        stuffed with stress my own intestine
        swells like a boiled sausage
        till it gets all the mustard and relish
        leaving the leavened bread
        the staff of life
        stuck with a red-hot

        as a creative person
        i try to be thankful
        for the sudden presence
        of this annoying intruder
        knowing that a gut full of anxiety
        can be a useful motivator
        and knowing also
        a bun all by itself
        would never make it at coney island
        and certainly
        i want to make it
        i'd love to be an oscar meyer weiner
        singing and dancing
        a real hot-dog!

but that doesn't mean i enjoy being eaten

A LOOSE END

         it's true i've put off
dealing
           with one aspect of my father's life
           a loose end so to speak
           perhaps because he died when i was so young
           and i remember him not so much as a person
           but more of a presence
                a feeling

         so it's not him that i must
finally
           get around to, rather the end of him
           he was forty-nine when he passed away
           i was twelve—and he seemed older than god then
           but now with me at forty-six i can see
                he was in his prime and his
                untimely

         death is what really has me
bothered
           the shadow of this event just ahead
           the date crossing my path—an open fracture
           in the shape of a question mark
           i ask myself
           could i ever be older than
                my father?

         and a kind of panic
fills me
           to break through the barrier

and find myself alone on the other side
without him
i think i'd rather die first
and in the next three years if i'm not careful
this could be the loaded gun that just might
      kill me

GEORGE BLANDA
(Song lyric)

in my forty seventh season
came a night i couldn't sleep
my weary eyes popped open
like i had a date to keep
and i stumbled through the darkness
fumbled for the light
my mind said it was morning
but the time said it was night

so i brewed a cup of coffee up
stewed around till dawn
till the boy who threw the paper
threw the paper on the lawn
the headlines were depressing
so i read the sporting green
and saw where old george blanda
hadn't made the team

now life can be a blessing
yes — and life can be a curse
and i know that i'll see better days
but nothing could be worse
than to watch a living legend
grow old and disappear
and to do it in the middle
of my forty seventh year

a lot of us went with him
as he slowly left the field
to empty out his locker

till it looked the way i feel
like george i'm pushing fifty
and time is marching on
but i feel as young as ever
with a little something wrong

he left me older than the oldest
player in the game
and it doesn't help a bit to know
he'll make the hall of fame
'cause they called the man an old man
and the old man was my peer
and it happened in the middle
of my forty seventh year

*Imagine the following sung by a mens
chorus using the* **Battle Hymn of
the Republic** *for the melody*

"Glory, glory, George Blanda.
Go tell the story of George Blanda.
Lord we're sorry that George Blanda,
George Blanda is gone!"

but this is more than just a tribute
to another gridiron great
i put it down for anyone
who thinks it's getting late
but perhaps you are a person
who is not a football fan
so i'll put it in another way
that you might understand

that i wonder where a **Catcher
In The Rye** goes when he's gone
and when bobby dylan gets here

will he still feel like a song?
there were flowers in the garbage
and nothing left to cheer
and it happened in the middle
of my forty seventh year

       life can be a blessing
       yes — and life can be a curse
       and i know that i'll see better days
       but nothing could be worse
       than to sink into an armchair
       (Phist!) cryin' in my beer
       and to do it in the middle
       of my forty seventh year

THE GREAT ESCAPE

if freedom is nothing more
than being able to choose your own cage
        as i suggest it is
then perhaps the fun comes
in being an escape artist

in recognizing the cage you are in
deciding how long you will settle for it
and then
when you want out
seeing how clever you are
at slipping through the wire

      perhaps the good life
          the full life
    is nothing more
    than every once in a while
    pulling yourself through a hole
        in the roof
    standing triumphantly
    looking down with a
        hot damn
            and then around
           with an
              oh shit!

Over 50

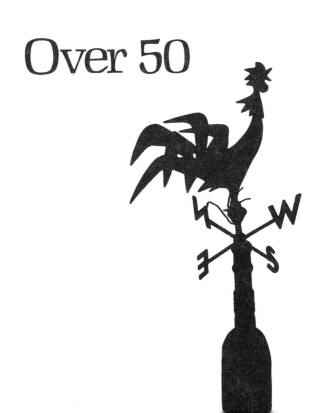

recently i have been going to you
as an old fool to a secret lover
and not unlike a tired salesman
bored with his territory
i have been giving in to temptation
sneaking off in the afternoon
for a quickie little nap
a diversion
always coming out of it with a start
a twinge of fear
telling myself
i shouldn't be here like this with you

but late in the evening
when the time is right
and what we do together is socially acceptable
shamelessly
i can give myself to you completely
        forgetting the past
        letting the future go
and oh
how i hate to leave you in the morning

sleep!
you have become an acceptable death
lovers of life — a warning

RELATIVITY

have you noticed
that everyone else's kid
seems able
to understand einstein's
theory of relativity?

while yours
can't seem to find the door

we laugh now

but not long ago
a father's misgivings
were kept locked away
on the third floor
like
idiot children

COMING HOME

the continuing story of a traveling salesman
continues
       this time
       we find him running
       out of an airport
       giftshop
       with a cap pistol
       and a doll
       a surprise for the kids
       but like oxfords
       hastily bought
                a size too small
(the kids i remembered
were not kids at all)

"i think i've been gone longer than i thought"
       cried
       old saint nick
       as ever ho-ho-hoing
       as ever coming and going
       giving the children puppies for christmas
       never there when the dog died

but it's okay dad
it's all right
they say
       there is no such thing
       as a bad parent
they say
       even people who batter their offspring

are doing the best
they know how to do

and you can tell that
to the boxes that were never opened

you can tell that to the shoes that pinch

FATHER COME LATELY

unopened as yet
the envelope turns in my hand
and
i suppose the flying wallendas can
but i never could stand at ease
watching my children
      play in the woods
      play in the trees
so certain was i that they would fall
and they did
and they didn't

but now that they have grown old
as i was then
out on their own
sending messages home
      as to where they are
      and how they've been
the envelope turns in my hand
and nothing has changed at all

ON THE MOUNTAIN

somewhere about a third of the way up
he came striding down the trail
and caught me unaware
a poet
staff in hand — naked — thin as a whip
wild gray hair framing the sunstained face
his bright eyes blue holes
                        and sky showing through

when he saw me resting there
he laughed out loud
        friend, he said
        i have been to the summit
                    and found nothing there
                    absolutely nothing
then laughing again
he went on down around the bend
                    and left me

with my brand new dayglow knapsack
ten dollar compass — waterproof boots
remembering how i'd sharpened my knife
till it shaved the hair
on the back of my wrist
preparing myself for almost anything but this

still i was young then
and it wasn't until i too
had run out of places to climb
                    that i began to wonder

where he was going and what he was after
                    laughing that way
and so turning around
                    i followed on down behind

and if i took you by surprise
this morning coming down the path
believe me i was only laughing at myself
                    sitting there

A MEMO FROM THE PAST

at twenty five you can't imagine
how frustrating it is to be over fifty
trying to explain something
to someone twenty five

to someone whose monday is two weeks
away from my next sunday

to someone on whose person things
have not begun growing and/or
started dropping off and falling out of

to someone who hasn't yet discovered
that being old feels exactly like
being young — with something wrong

and so for those of you who maintain
chronological age is irrelevant
i have prepared a statement
to be opened and read the day
they themselves turn fifty
a memo that goes:

> greetings know it all
> and don't say i didn't tell you so."

(The anticipation of such an upcoming event is incentive
enough to keep me alive for another twenty five years.)

THE HANDYMAN

it's autumn
i feel it in my bones
and other places

it's autumn
i can no longer afford
to own a cricket lighter
having thrown too much away already

it's autumn
time to maintain
a not-very-
exciting prospect
for those who remain
in a springtime/summertime
frame of mind
but there is more to maintenance
than a drop of oil
        a dab of glue
a thing gathers value and interest
as you rub off the new
so go to work on what you've got

it's autumn
and according to my wife
an old chest
becomes a priceless antique
only
if it gets a good going over
at least twice a week

THE QUALITY OF LOVE

in the throws of the affair
i was surprised to learn
i could love two women with intensity
at the same time
one with whom i'd spent many years
and one recently met

now the quality of these loves
is best described by the difference
in my bathroom behavior — toilet procedure
        at home
though the room was occupied
(my wife in the tub)
when ya gotta go
ya gotta go — and i always went
        but in an apartment near chicago
i would carefully close the door
run the water and turn the fan on

during this time
if a doctor had informed me
i had but six months to live
looking back
i think i would have chosen the apartment
for the first three months
but i know now
i would have wished to go home
to die with someone who knows
just how full of crap
i really am

WAITING WITH A FRIEND
DYING OF CANCER

forty-nine and waiting
and what for
the bottom line

back in act one — scene one
it was obvious
we were waiting to see what would happen
but deeper into the drama
we recognize the antagonist
and realize there will be no "surprise" ending
which would seem to make it a farce

so i'll go with that awhile
and tell about a comic
who built a career around a rickety ladder
and he was funny enough
to make us smile and forget

being silly is a noble occupation
so i fashioned some tom foolery of my own
i really didn't know what i was doing
but i loved watching you go for it
coming by
gawking like a tourist
slowing down for a better view
then — WHAM!
i'd be there with a slapstick
clowning around in the death scene
doing pratfalls
waiting for the laughs

that's it!

that's what we're all waiting for
the end is always there
you can count on it
but the laughs
are few and far between

(I had reached the point in my life where I knew I was
waiting for something and just assumed that the something
was death. But while working through the above I realized I
was waiting not for death, but for the next moment that
would make life worth living. Like many men my age I had
lost faith and that loss of faith had come close to killing me.)

THE NOUVEAU RURAL

it's why we live here
terry said

this last 4th of july
when we awoke to a water tower
drained dry
useless faucets
and a mile and a half of empty PVC
the mountainside went wild
      waving wrenches
      running beside the pipe
      bumping into each other
      Mack Sennett
      looking for leaks in the line
and for awhile
till the toilets flushed again
      at least
there was meaning
and direction
      in the lives
      of eight
      middle-aged men

THE BALD POEM

getting a little thin on top
aren't you sport?

my neanderthal brothers
get a kick
out of razzing me this way

and i am going bald
but what would you have me do?
nurture and cultivate a sideburn
till it hangs down like a house plant
like a long trailing fern
to rake across my barren crown

or would you prefer a transplant
my naked pate a parade ground
where rows of foreign follicles
stand like the michigan state
marching band
poised to play the national anthem

perhaps a toupee?
a saucy little pompadour
that when not in use
lies around the house like a lap dog
like the dusty pelt of a pekingese
which I suspect smells of musty tapestry

do this to my head?
no way — not me!

like the granite dome
that presides over yosemite valley
i would not be what i am
with trees

my scalp is bare
but gentlemen look at it this way
we all begin with roughly
the same number of hormones

      and if you want to blow yours
      growing hair —

BURNOUT (A MISNOMER)

burn-out
you've seen the results
in the shop on the shelf
row after row of grey empty faces
with nothing happening in the glassy eyes
except
a little surface reflection

burn-out
you know the symptoms ...
a history of dependable service
then suddenly for no reason things go dark
and you're a dead piece of furniture
waiting
to be removed from the living room

burn-out
the psychological repairman said
and shrugged and shook his head
having checked everything
except the cord
which of course
                       was disconnected

in a word unplugged

and to think
i nearly went to the dump myself
because someone less than a poet
trying to describe a condition

came up with a misleading term
clearly
a case of burn-out demands a second opinion
and this is mine

        find an outlet
        and if the cord doesn't reach
        move the set

AN ASTRONAUT

is it enough
to be the attendant pumping gas
into a car driven by someone who works
the night shift at a factory making parts
for one small component in a rocket engine?
>   no
>   not when you want to fly

so let's have another space shot
only this time
not a carefully picked highly trained
physically fit super intelligent astronaut
this time
chosen by national lottery
an unqualified overweight
over forty beer drinking sports fan like me
someone who still doesn't know
how they go to the john up there

what a moment it would be
the world watching as i'm stuffed into a silver suit
strapped onto a capsule couch
slapped on the helmet
bolted in
counted down
and blasted off
sent up into the night — into the stars
out — so far
i'd give anything to be back where i am
right now

A NORMAN KING

middle-aged and bored beyond belief
i went into the brush today
and like a child made myself a clearing

with grub hoe and axe
i fought the undergrowth
and did battle with the greasewood and genista
the going wasn't easy
the bushes striking — slashing back
until the branches brought me crashing down
a whip-like blow across the face

  thanks
  i needed that

then cursing in childish rage
i rise a norman king
to chop and hack
at the very root of my lethargy

take that and that and that ... and
slowly — grudgingly
the enemy falls back
until at last i have myself
a piece of open ground

to rest on — to lie upon
and watch the sky from

  listen the wind is cheering

OVER FIFTY

deep into autumn
the third period
i have discovered
that winning the game
is not what is important

what is important though
is
that i look good
while losing

BOOKS . . .

Also available on order, through local bookstores that use R.R. Bowker Company BOOKS IN PRINT catalogue system.

☐ **STARK NAKED** *(1980)*
  by Ric Masten
43 poems, 7 songs, 5 photographs. 110 pages. ISBN 931104-1.

☐ **Paperback $4.95**   ☐ **Hardcover $9.95**

☐ **VOICE OF THE HIVE** *(1978)*
  by Ric Masten
54 poems, 6 songs, 104 pages. ISBN 931104-02-5.

Paperback $4.95

☐ **SPEAKING POEMS** *(Revised 1979)*
  by Ric Masten
58 poems, 4 songs, 8 woodcuts, 112 pages. ISBN 931104-06-8.

Paperback $4.95

☐ **HIS & HERS** *(1974)*
  by Ric and Billie Barbara Masten
39 poems, the Relationship Contract, text, 80 pages.
ISBN 931104-01-7.   **Paperback $3.95**

☐ **OWNING THE BEAST AND THE BAD GIRL** *(1975)*
  by Billie Barbara Masten
25 poems, 40 pages. ISBN 931104-07-6.

Paperback $3.50

RECORD ALBUMS . . .

☐ *Ric Masten singing*
  LET IT BE A DANCE *(1979)*
12 songs with Bluegrass accompaniment. Stereo SF-1002.

Price $5.95

BROADSIDES . . . Price .50

Single sheets printed on colored stock. 8½"x11", suitable for framing.

☐ The Warty Frog   ☐ Let It Be a Dance
☐ The Second Half   ☐ The Homesick Snail

☐ PUBLICITY PAMPHLETS

☐ Ric Masten in Concert . . . ☐ On the College Campus.
☐ In the High School . . . ☐ In the Middle School.
☐ In the Elementary . . . ☐ In the Church . . . ☐ On Relationships.
☐ Honorarium and Fee Schedule.

- -

CHECKS MADE OUT TO

SUNFLOWER INK
Palo Colorado Canyon
Carmel, CA 93923

ORDER $_____

6% SALES TAX (CA. RES.) _____

SHIPPING & HANDLING $____$1.00____

TOTAL $_____

Name _____

Address_____

City _____ State _____ Zip _____